TEACHING TIPS
&
TECHNIQUES

Revised

by
Kathryn Stout, B.S.Ed., M.Ed.

HELP FOR THE
HOMESCHOOLING PARENT

A DESIGN-A-STUDY BOOK

Other titles by Kathryn Stout

Books

Comprehensive Composition
Critical Conditioning
Guides to History Plus
Maximum Math
Natural Speller
Science Scope
The Maya

Audiocassettes

A Chronological Unit Approach to History
Developing Attitudes and Habits
How to Teach Composition
Make It Easy on Yourself
Math That Makes Sense
Strategies for Teaching and Learning Spelling
Teaching English: What's Essential?
Teaching Kids to Think
Teaching Reading, Spelling, & Critical Thinking
Teaching Teenagers to Think Critically
Teaching Tips That Really Work

Current listings and prices available from
Design-A-Study, 408 Victoria Ave., Wilmington, DE 19804
Phone/Fax: (302) 998-3889

Website: www.designastudy.com

E-mail: kathryn@designastudy.com

Cover Design by Richard B. Stout and Ted Karwowski.

©1991 Revised Edition 1999

Published by Design-A-Study, 408 Victoria Avenue, Wilmington, DE 19804-2124 Printed in the U.S.A.

ISBN 1- 891975-07-2

Library of Congress Catalog Card Number: 99-094887

TABLE OF CONTENTS

INTRODUCTION

Before you try the ideas in this guide, you may want to know just whose advice you are taking—I would. Everything you find here has been "field tested"—not as a researcher, but as a teacher who has always looked for ways to get through to kids. I would hunt for ideas, try them out, and keep anything that brought children closer to a love of learning and a real understanding of a subject.

I've been teaching as long as I can remember. In elementary school, the teacher would send me classmates that needed help with a math problem or a report. After school I played teacher with my neighborhood friends. During my senior year in high school I spent an hour each day as a teacher's aid, occasionally teaching a lesson in history, and in college, the professor often asked me to demonstrate algebra problems when the class seemed confused by his explanations.

My teaching became official once I graduated from the University of Delaware with a Bachelor of Science degree in elementary education. Over the next few years I taught various grades in public school and worked on my master's degree in special education during the summers.

Upon receiving my master's degree I became a "troubleshooter" (S&E Interventionist) for a school district, working in five elementary and two private schools. Teachers contacted me for help with students having especially troublesome problems in class, or just to have another observer to help them decide what the source of a problem might be. I would observe, meet with the student and sometimes the parents, offer plans

7

for the teacher or parents to try, and/or work with the student on a regular basis.

The federal grant funding my position expired and I spent the next few years testing, teaching special education, and helping set up a special education program. Summers, I tutored students from ages six to seventeen in a variety of subjects.

All of these experiences convinced me that home education would be the best option for my own children. Any student thrives when taught one-to-one or in a small group, but schools require teachers to serve twenty-five to thirty students with a wide range of backgrounds, skills, and emotional needs. I didn't want to take the chance that my own children would become bored and lose their love of learning.

Although I worked with both of my children before they were school age, my daughter went to a half-day kindergarten program and to first grade because my husband hoped it would "cure" her shyness. She already knew how to read, and at the first grade open house we realized she had already accomplished the year's objectives. Therefore, I continued projects and enjoyable learning activities with her after school.

Attendance in public school not only did not alter her shyness, but it made her sullen. She has a few good memories of kindergarten (although I remember daily tears when I put her on the bus) but merely endured first grade. Within a year of being taught entirely at home, she blossomed. I mention this for anyone that may have a "clingy" child that everyone thinks should be sent off for "his own good." Schooled at home through high school, Clea grew into a confident and sociable adult. At 17 she traveled to Russia with Josh McDowell ministries. At 18 she entered the University of

Delaware, where she graduated with honors. Currently, she is a scholarship student at Widener University School of Law. More importantly, she is a strong Christian committed to serving God.

Unlike his sister, my son Christopher was born sociable. Because there were no neighborhood playmates available, he eagerly went to the half-day kindergarten at the public school nearby. We started him in first grade because I was planning to have back surgery. I didn't, and wish we'd taken him out instead of insisting he finish out the year. He was a nervous wreck in the all-day, textbook environment, and only the projects at home offset his misery. Once he was taught entirely at home, his need to socialize was met through his participation in church activities, various sports programs at the local YMCA, and involvement in music—performing on the violin in orchestras and chamber music groups. He also invited friends over for a day or a sleepover as often as possible. Christopher now attends the University of Southern California on a USC Presidential Scholarship. A committed Christian, he plans to make a positive impact on society as a filmmaker.

Throughout the homeschool years I also served other families as an educational consultant, which I continue to do. I offer here the accumulation of my experiences.

GETTING STARTED

Forget your past as a student in a typical classroom. Do not try to turn your home into a mini-public school with textbooks and desks that your children will have to use six hours a day. Remember that schools are not run as they are because it is the best way to educate, but because control must be maintained over a large number of students.

Relax and enjoy your children and you will discover that real learning can take place without the stern voice and the drudgery of endless workbook assignments. Begin by choosing concepts and skills you want your children to master. Completing a book or program may (or may not) be the result of working toward those goals, but should never be your objective. Just by making that adjustment in your thinking you'll realize that learning can be accomplished in all kinds of interesting ways.

Too often, an objective is chosen and then followed by a long list of activities that will enable students to accomplish that single objective. While this may be necessary on occasion to build mastery in an especially weak area, there is a much more effective and efficient approach: **assign an activity or project that incorporates several objectives.** For example, assigning spelling words to be copied for handwriting practice combines what are usually two lessons into one.

Another effective and efficient method is to cover objectives in several different subject areas while focusing study on one activity or topic: a **project approach** or **unit study**. Children enjoy this method and usually retain concepts, skills, and information longer than with the traditional method of isolating every subject. It also allows you to teach children of different ages together fairly easily.

How to Plan a Unit Study

1. Choose a focus for your unit study. A work of fiction (literature-based unit studies), or a topic in history or science are popular approaches. The topic, not the supporting activities, provides the common ground for students of various ages.

   A project can also serve as the focus that provides the common ground. In that case as well, supporting activities may vary to adjust to the needs of each student. Examples of projects include putting on a play or newscast, publishing a newspaper, building a model or display, and developing their own business—even selling lemonade require measuring, handling money, sign making, and preparing a presentation.

2. Choose activities that will not only increase knowledge about the topic, but also provide practice in skills and concepts taught in several other subject areas. It is not necessary to try to force a connection to a subject. Anything not covered in one unit can be covered either in another study, or with materials that isolate the subject. The concepts and skills most

frequently practiced in unit study activities are art, composition, and reading comprehension.

3. Choose activities that suit the age, ability, and learning style of each child. Because older children should never be held back or younger children pushed ahead in order to have everyone working together, it is important to adjust the activities chosen in order to suit each child involved. This can be done by assigning different activities, or by using different materials for the same activities. In the first case, a young child may be asked to listen to a story and act it out while an older child reads a different story and writes a book review. In the second case, both children could be assigned literature to read and a follow-up composition, but given different books to accommodate their varying reading levels.

4. Record the objectives being covered in each unit study. This allows the teacher to keep track of progress and avoid assigning activities in subject books "just to be sure." Design-A-Study books can be used to determine objectives as well as to record the dates on which those objectives were covered.

A Sample

The topic of a unit could be the study of a tribe of North American Indians. While children of different ages would all be involved in this study, each would be working on skills appropriate to his own ability. All students could read or listen to a variety of fiction (literature) and nonfiction books (history, reading comprehension), write or dictate a composition about some aspect of Indian life, be shown, asked to find, or required to make a map illustrating locations of tribes (geography), make and decorate a drum (art, music), and so on.

Since activities are suited to the age and capability of each child, **different projects can be assigned to each student and then brought back to the group to be shared**. The five-year-old could display and play the drum he made, the ten-year-old could research customs of the Sioux and present his findings while dressed in costume (practicing research skills that would be too advanced for his younger siblings), and the fourteen-year-old could compare the Sioux with another tribe of Plains Indians, displaying posters, models, artifacts, or maps as he gives his presentation—accomplishing more objectives, in-cluding compare/contrast writing, then is necessary for the others.

They could also (or instead) **work on a project together.** The project itself would involve skills in various subject areas. For example, planning the dimensions and building a teepee would involve math skills, and possibly even physical science skills. History books would be used to learn about the materials used to build teepees, and any decorative markings. Older students could help the younger students as they work together. The experience could be completed by having students sit inside the teepee and share Indian tales they have read (literature) and/or written in imitation of original Native American tales (composition).

During a study of ancient Greece, my children worked together writing and performing (with friends) a talk show in which they interviewed various Greek gods. Their questions and answers were based on each god's involvement in Homer's *The Iliad*, which I had read to them. They also wrote and acted out their own commercials using information from an earlier study of propaganda techniques.

While they were involved in this project, I was able to check off (in the Design-A-Study books) the specific objectives they were practicing in history, reading comprehension, and composition. Because it is not necessary to teach a particular period of history or specific literature in a given grade, my children were able to work together despite the almost four-year difference in their ages.

Teaching Essential Skills

Standard objectives are part of all curriculum packages and may be found in their teaching guides. Lists may also be obtained from the education department of many states. If you would like to have explanations of the objectives, lists that are grouped by topic (not just by grade) so that you can teach the same objective more easily to several children, as well as suggestions for teaching the subject, then you should find the Design-A-Study subject books by this author especially helpful.

Once you choose the objectives you want to focus on for a given period of time, select materials and teaching methods appropriate for each child's age and learning style. Those materials should always be treated as tools, never as the teacher or as the final authority about what to cover, or how and when to cover objectives. Then you are free to adjust the pace and change your approach as the need arises.

If you cover a topic with children of various ages, some may be too young to understand all of the concepts. This should not hinder their participation, simply go over those concepts again when those children are older. Any skills missed by the younger children can also be included in other lessons that year or at a later date. On the other hand, not all children need to participate in every unit study. Older students might study state history together while younger children spend extra time learning to read. For example, my daughter completed a study of Delaware when my son was six and uninterested. At ten, he could focus on a state study while she, a teenager, worked independently on a study of careers. Together, we worked on projects in science.

Whether using unit studies or projects for one child or several, it remains necessary to **teach essential skills in phonics, spelling, math, and typing directly**, using specific materials that allow complete focus. Any weak areas in other subjects should also be targeted for periodic practice using resources that focus on that particular weakness. By individualizing practice in these areas, the child is able to develop at his own pace, relieved of stress and competition.

Implementing a unit study approach to cover at least a few subjects frees you to individualize or bring everyone together as much or as little as you desire. And, it saves money. You can use the library as a primary resource, avoiding the expense of textbooks for every child in every subject. Instead, specific needs can be targeted and workbooks, texts, and supplies can be purchased to meet those needs. That means science kits, exciting books and videos, games, geoboards, and anything else that appeals to your children can be used to meet objectives instead of being left for "after school." No more feeling guilty when you all have a good time!

What About High School?

While teenagers may be too busy or simply uninterested in participating in activities with younger children, they can still be taught with a unit study approach to some degree. That is, objectives in reading comprehension—including research skills, composition, and grammar—can be taught while focusing on content in history and literature. Some literature chosen for study can be set in the period of history or the culture being studied, or be written by an author of the period or culture. Reading writings—whether complete or merely excerpts—that influenced a society helps students develop a greater depth of understanding. Their compositions should then reflect a growing ability to analyze. (*Guides to History Plus* provides a list of books by period to supplement American and world history and includes questions for discussion or composition to encourage analysis.)

While other high school subjects are generally best taught separately, it is still important to work toward mastery of objectives, not simply completion of a text or packet of information. Therefore, resources and methods should be chosen for their usability to the student.

At this level subjects increase in detail and more is expected of the student than simple recall. Students still need a teacher and discussion. Tutors, video and satellite programs can all be helpful. Resource choices include texts and workbooks that cover the most essential content and skills only and use a vocabulary suited to a third or fourth grade reading level as well as materials suitable for students preparing for college and everything in-between. Choosing all materials from one company may seem efficient but should never be done unless it appears to be the best choice for the student. Frequently, it is more effective to choose materials subject by subject, looking over resources available from several companies.

Students of all ages should find learning fun at least some of the time. Obviously, persevering to develop greater ability in any subject or skill can also be tedious. However, it is the enjoyment of learning new things and feeling a sense of accomplishment that keeps the balance. The approach to teaching described here is eclectic because the focus is on meeting the needs of the student. It is effective for that same reason. Certainly it is easier to do the routine and necessary when we can look forward to something enjoyable. And what is considered enjoyable varies from student to student.

GETTING ORGANIZED

- Keep supplies in places that are accessible *to your children.* Allow them to get whatever they need as it is needed, and return reusable items when finished. This will ultimately save you time and effort, as well as help your children become more independent in their studies.

- Use a notebook for planning and note taking; bits of paper are likely to get lost before you have a chance to copy them.

- Have supplies on hand ahead of time so that projects aren't interrupted. The following items are basics that should always be accessible:

  ☑ A globe.

  ☑ Laminated maps of the world and the United States.

   Mine are stapled to a wall. It's amazing how familiar my kids became with geography just from looking at the maps to satisfy their own curiosity.

  ☑ Atlas.

  ☑ Almanac. *(It doesn't have to be current.)*

☑ **Dictionaries.**

- Children's dictionary for young students.

- Merriam-Webster adult dictionary.

☑ **A set of encyclopedias.**

Worldbook is especially readable for elementary and junior high school students. I bought a set at a thrift shop for six dollars.

☑ **Thesaurus.**

You may want a version for younger children, but be sure to have the adult Roget's Thesaurus. This is a great reference to help students expand their vocabulary. Encourage them to use more precise words, but explain the connotations of the choices. Too often students simply pick a word from the list to try something different without realizing that the word is actually inappropriate in their context. This is the reason some writers discourage the use of a thesaurus. For example, while "bystander" is given as a synonym for "witness," it would not be correct to write, "The judge ordered the bystander to answer the defense attorney's question."

☑ **Shelves that are accessible.**

Fill the shelves with a variety of books that will appeal to the ages of the students. Notice the layout and print size of books they tend to choose at the library to help guide your purchases.

☑ Table or desk suitable to the student's size. A study carrel for those having difficulty maintaining attention.

Young children will do more on their own if they have a table and chair that suits their size. While a hard, smooth floor may be used for drawing when working on some projects, handwriting, typing, and work requiring more precise drawing should be taught and practiced with children seated appropriately.

If it is necessary to seat young students at the kitchen or dining room table, place something on the chair as necessary so that the children sit with their chests above the table surface and their arms in a comfortable writing position. Place a box or other support under their feet. Dangling feet can sap energy.

A study carrel is a two- or three-sided screen that sits on a table or desktop to block the student's view of visual distractions. These can be made easily out of cardboard, or purchased. (Refer to Calloway House in the suppliers' list.)

☑ Balls.

All types and sizes. A beach ball is good for indoor games with young children.

☑ Blocks.

- Large, lightweight building blocks for the young.

- Smaller construction blocks.

- Manipulatives for math activities.

☑ Boxes.

- Large boxes to be made into a house or puppet stage for elementary age children.

- Shoe boxes for dioramas.

☑ Dress up clothing.

Hats, scarves, robes, and jewelry are especially versatile props for impromptu and planned performances.

☑ General Supplies.

- Crayons, markers, colored pencils, number two pencils. Use large sizes for younger children to grip and control their strokes more easily.

- Erasers.

- Ruler, compass, protractor, string or yarn.

- Scissors for both adults and children.

- Hole punch.

- Scotch tape, white glue, glue stick.

- Stapler, brass fasteners (to put together booklets).

- Magnifying glass.

- Clay, or homemade dough.

- Watercolor paints, tempera, or poster paints paint brushes of various sizes.

- Drawing paper in various sizes, tracing paper, and construction paper in a variety of colors, poster board.
- Handwriting paper that includes the dotted middle line for ages 5 – 10.

☑ Optional supplies for projects.

Popsicle sticks, Styrofoam balls in assorted sizes, scraps of material, yarn in a variety of colors, glitter, and stickers

Suppliers

Following are a few companies that carry such classroom supplies as furniture, organizers, study carrels, handwriting paper, pencil grips, and art materials.

Calloway House
Phone 1-800-233-0290   www.callowayhouse.com
451 Richardson Dr., Lancaster, PA 17603

National School Products
Phone 1-800-627-9393
101 East Broadway, Maryville, TN 37804
Request the catalog "Classroom Resources."

J.L. Hammett Co.
Phone 1-800-333-4600   www.hammett.com
P.O. Box 660420, Dallas, TX 75266-0420

SCHEDULES AND LESSON PLANS

Have a schedule. You can be flexible within a schedule, and you can change your schedule as you see a need—but have one, nevertheless. It's amazing how many little household things can become distractions and how the school day can disappear without a bit accomplished if there's no established routine.

The schedule should allow time for the children's chores and any outside school activities (music lessons, sports, church functions) as well as the time allotted for school.

Here's one of the many schedules we used:

7:30 – 8:30 A.M.   Kids get up and prepare for the day.

They wash, dress, make their beds, and, usually, fix their own breakfast.

8:30 – 9:00 A.M.   Devotions

They are required to meet in the living room promptly at 8:30 a.m.

9:00 - 11:00 A.M.   School

11:00 - 11:30 A.M.   Lunch and free time

11:30 - 3:00 P.M.	School
3:00 - 3:30 P.M.	Free time
3:30 - 4:30 P.M.	School

Music practice and music theory lessons (both play instruments) were included during hours marked "School."

4:30 - 8:30 P.M.

Evenings varied. When sports or music activities were scheduled, the children were assigned fewer chores so that they would still have some time to themselves.

| 8:30 - 9:00 P.M. | Kids get ready for bed. |

This included picking up their bedrooms and leaving a neat bathroom.

| 9:00 – 9:30 P.M. | Read aloud. |

Don't stop reading out loud because your children know how to read. Children look forward to this time. It's also an incentive to get their work done.

Be sure to schedule in your own quiet time. At various times I used their nap time, an hour in the evening after they were in bed, and the hour in the morning when they were preparing for school.

I won't pretend that we were always on schedule or that the kids always managed to keep their bedrooms and the bathroom neat. (Notice that the rest of the house hasn't even been mentioned....) But, we did achieve those goals more often than if there had been no schedule at all.

Kids need to have a sense of order—not to be confused with monotony—and an understanding of what is expected of them. This includes knowing the consequences if they don't do whatever they've been told to do. If you don't follow through, they will assume nothing will happen.

To get my kids to the point of meeting me in the living room at 8:30 each morning, they missed a few breakfasts and spent some lunch breaks doing their morning tasks. Anything not done had to wait until lunch break, even getting dressed. They looked forward to playing and certainly didn't want to waste any of their break with chores, so it didn't take long to get into the routine.

As they grew, each one had been instructed, step-by-step, as to how to wash, dress, hang up clothes, make the bed, and so on. **Never expect more than you have taught specifically, one-on-one.** Remember that all instruction must be followed up. Check their work to encourage a job well done.

When projects and appointments left us with unbearable clutter (and I developed a fairly high tolerance since we are all project people), I altered my lesson plans. I read out loud (history, science, and literature) while they picked up, did dishes, swept floors, and dusted. We even managed to paint my son's bedroom while learning about the Vikings by taking turns being the reader or a painter.

LESSON PLANS

Before purchasing curriculum materials, imagine your child using the product on a regular basis. Can you envision a willing worker? If not, even though the product may appear to be easy for you to implement—no lesson plans to develop, for instance—will you actually end up putting lots of effort into making your child do the work? That can be much more tiring in the long run.

Once the resources have passed that test, try to create a mental picture of the flow of the day rather than scheduling based on your desire to get schoolwork "out of the way." As you think it through, you may "see" one child fidgeting because he has had to sit at quiet tasks too long. Now you can change the order of your activities before a problem ever arises.

The actual day may not go according to plan, but, again, flexibility is easier within a framework, and you will gradually achieve more goals if you have an overall sense of structure. It will also be easier to handle those crazy days when the kids fuss, the plumbing backs up, and every salesman seems to have your phone number.

Keep the following points in mind while planning your school schedule:

Maintain Attention

1. The younger the child, the shorter the attention span.

Up to age seven the rule of thumb is one minute of attention per year in his age. This does not mean that the subject must be changed every few minutes, only that some sort of interaction is necessary to regain the child's focus. It would be unrealistic planning to expect a young child to work at a task without supervision for 45 minutes. Refer to the section "What to Expect" for guidelines.

2. **The younger the child, the less time he will be able to spend on anything independently.**

However, by spending time showing him how, and guiding him to do, a young child can become independent in many areas sooner than other children of the same age who are not given this sort of specific instruction

3. **Change and movement can refocus attention and stimulate learning.**

Alternate quiet, sit-down activities with those that allow kids movement and/or excitement. For example, work one-on-one on a phonic lesson for 10 minutes, (quiet) then play a game, or have them point out objects in the room that begin with the "b" sound (movement).

While taking a nature walk (movement), stop to examine a leaf or bug, asking questions that will require close observation to answer (quiet).

4. **Include exercise breaks.**

Too often physical education is pushed to the bottom of the "to-do" list in favor of the academic. But, by incorporating organized physical activity into the school day, you can actually increase your children's ability to focus on and retain information. Studies by teachers in classrooms indicate that hard exercise for twenty minutes three times a day improved the ability of the students to maintain focus on schoolwork after the exercise.

Children also need to build strength, balance, coordination, and flexibility as part of their overall development. All of these physical aspects affect them in ways that can either help or hinder academic areas. For example, if muscles are weak, students may sit with poor posture, leading to fatigue more quickly when they must read or write. With fatigue comes difficulty in main-taining concentration, resulting in the student becoming restless, or simply falling asleep. However, overall weakness or lack of co-ordination can also lead to difficulties in manipulating objects, reading left to right easily, or following sentences on a page. This is one reason programs for young children incorporate a variety of physical activities, and why many children with learning disabilities benefit from physical and occupational therapy.

Since vigorous exercise sustained for at least twenty minutes at a time also helps (temporarily) decrease symptoms of anxiety, depression, and stress according to various health studies throughout the late 1980's and 90's, exercising with your kids should help you maintain the pace required to be both mother and teacher.

5. Don't allow the clock to rule the day.

Remember to be flexible within your planning. Allow students to continue with something while interest is high, or stop when it is obvious that they have reached their limit with an activity—that is, they are daydreaming, have become tired, or are easily distracted.

How much a student can accomplish in a day depends partly on how much the teacher is able to shift him from quiet to active participation. Older students can work for an hour before a change (sometimes more, if they are interested in what they are doing). Youngsters may require change every ten minutes. The shift does not have to be to a different subject, just a change in their involvement. Software often maintains a child's interest longer than a workbook page covering the same objective because of the many shifts between reading or listening and responding. This is also why discussions maintain interest and focus longer than lectures.

Young children are likely to exhaust you before themselves. Provide a variety of creative play materials in order to assure yourself that they are still learning when you leave them on their own. For example:

- Puzzles.
- Parquetry blocks and pattern cards.
- Area equipped for playing house.
- Books with corresponding audiocassettes to listen to the story while looking at the book.

Provide Practice That Builds Understanding

6. Establish priorities in areas of strength and weakness.

Education is not about memorizing the most information. It is about shaping a child's character, developing his abilities, and helping him overcome any obstacles that may be in his path because of weaknesses—whatever they may be. Therefore, it is important to address areas of weakness and to develop natural abilities.

Begin by listing academic and physical difficulties and note any concerns related to the child's behavior. It is not necessary to work toward improvement in all areas at once—that could be overwhelming. However, a specific plan should be made for each area at some point, rather than assuming time alone will bring about change.

Academic weaknesses may include difficulty in learning to read phonetically, inability to grasp main ideas (reading comprehension), poor organization skills, sloppy handwriting, inability to retain spelling words beyond the tests, difficulty retaining an understanding of math concepts, difficulty memorizing math facts, and so on. Set a goal within an area that can be met successfully within several weeks. The student will be reaching the larger goal by accomplishing smaller goals one at a time. At each stage, use materials that are suitable to the student's learning style, or adapt them. Increase the amount of daily practice, working the student to the point of saturation.

Physical limitations may involve weak motor skills, vision or speech difficulties, hearing loss, allergies, or disabilities that require special attention or interfere with schooling by causing fatigue or inability to concentrate. These areas generally require ongoing treatment and must be considered when selecting resources and scheduling lessons. Occasionally, you may want to schedule additional time in order to experiment with a new technique or try a new resource. Look for alternatives that allow the student to learn how to compensate for any long-lasting weakness. For example, if motor skills are unlikely to improve to the degree that handwriting will ever be neat, use a mature signature as the goal, and teach the student to type. If typing proves impossible, use software that allows the student to simply speak in order to have a written composition.

Behaviors that need to be changed could include inability to stay focused, rushing through a task without concern that it be done correctly, fear of new experiences, excessive shyness or bossiness around other children, acting too impulsively or too cautiously, or other inappropriate actions. Target a behavior and decide on a method to employ consistently. After a few weeks, decide whether or not that method has been effective and should be continued. If so, it should become part of the routine until it appears that it is no longer effective. If not, you may want to try a new method immediately, or choose to wait until you have had time to look for more possibilities.

List areas of strength—that is, abilities and/or interests. For example, interest in music, art, and/or sports even without ability can be used as a key to choosing an approach that will draw the student into a subject. Including something that interests the student offsets the tediousness of working on areas of weakness.

Talent in any of these areas should be developed. This will encourage self-confidence. It will also provide some balance against the discouragement that so often accompanies effort in overcoming weaknesses.

It may seem as if this approach will result in leaving educational gaps, since it may not be possible to cover everything in a packaged curriculum and follow these suggestions as well. However, packaged programs provide regular review and tend to cover a great deal without depth—requiring more memorization than experience. It is possible to cover all the objectives thoroughly as long as you don't try to do it all at once. By deciding on priorities, instead of focusing on completing a package, you will be building a strong foundation. Students that develop skills and understanding will not require as much review later, and will be capable of absorbing greater amounts of information in upper grades.

I would plan generally for the year, targeting priorities in areas of strengths and weaknesses, and then take time every two or three months to refine these plans. By using the Design-A-Study subject books as a framework and penciling in the student's initials and the date next to objectives as they were covered, I could quickly note areas not previously covered or in need of review. (Be sure to record reviews too!) This and reference to my daily notes of work completed—which included lists of videos, field trips, projects, and books read—helped me determine areas of focus for the next few months.

7. **Adjust your expectations to suit the age, personality, and past performances of the student.**

In other words, each student should be treated as an individual by beginning with whatever he needs to know, despite his age, teaching him at a pace he can handle, and using the method that best suits him.

Too often we expect children to work independently because we want them to, not because they are actually capable of independence. Age, maturity, personality, learning style, and approaches used in teaching all influence the development of independence in learning.

Students must be encouraged to learn for its own sake. That is, they should want to know, understand, and be able to do. If a student thinks of work as something to complete just to get a grade—and, especially if he doesn't care what that grade is—he has lost any enthusiasm for learning that will contribute to working productively on his own.

It is important that a student not become discouraged because he sees himself as failing, or "behind," or become lazy because he is "ahead." Instead, the student should focus on where he wants to go and how to get there. This isn't as difficult as is sounds.

- When you spend time tutoring each child in basic skills such as phonics, math, and spelling, use aids to help the student see, hear, and do (touch). Begin at the level of his understanding, not age, and progress as he is able.

- Use the student's interest frequently as a key to begin exploring an area, and expand from there. For example, an allergy to wheat required one student to eat alternative grains. Friends refused to try her alternatives despite assurances that they tasted good. When it was time to learn how to plan and carry out a science experiment, the student decided to prove that using grains other than wheat did not result in a less tasty product. She baked cupcakes made with wheat flour and others made with rice flour, and then took a survey, asking several questions about the taste of each. Graphing the final results also incorporated math skills—a subject she found difficult. Because of her interest in the topic, she was motivated to work on all aspects of the project.

- Projects and unit studies that involve children of different ages allow each to participate according to his own ability while sharing in the overall result. This can be very motivating to struggling or young students.

  For example, if you are teaching children ages 4, 8, and 11, the older two could work together to write a short play while the four-year-old offered ideas for names of the characters and colored drawings to be used for puppets. Then they can all use the puppets to perform. The four-year-old feels respected and important because of his participation with the others, who can prompt him in his performance, if need be, so the play goes smoothly.

Or, students could study a common topic by having each child find the answer to a specific question appropriate to his age. Each would then present that information to the group using a visual aid he chooses (holding up pictures in books) or creates (posters, charts, models, etc.).

8. **Ask yourself: "What can I have them do to understand this lesson?" and "What can I have them do to practice, review, or apply the concepts or skills I want to teach?"**

We all learn best when we can see and hear and do. That's one reason manipulatives are important in learning math, and experiments are a necessary part of science.

"Doing" does not have to be complicated, time-consuming, or expensive to be effective. Here are a few easy ideas that kids enjoy:

☑ Movement to indicate an opinion.

During a discussion or review, have children stand if they agree or if they think a statement is true, and sit when they disagree, or think it is false. For variety, substitute movements for sit and stand: jump, bend, run in place, and so on.

☑ Looking through books for ideas or illustrations to share.

☑ Building a model.

☑ Art activities: drawing, coloring, and crafts.

Popular activities which can be used to cover objectives in various subjects include:

- Drawing or completing maps.

- Making posters to illustrate the topic of a presentation.

- Designing covers to turn their own stories into books.

☑ Playing games.

Games should cover specific objectives. They can provide an alternative form of practice, replacing a workbook page, for instance, or they can provide review to keep skills polished.

For example, comprehension in reading and math require **deductive reasoning**. The following board games available in most toy stores are inexpensive and can be used to build reasoning skills:

- *Battleship* (ages 7+) by Milton Bradley.

- *Chess.*

- *Clue* (ages 8+) or *Clue Junior* (ages 5+) by Parker Brothers.

- *Concentration* (ages 10+) by Endless Games.

- *Connect 4* (ages 7+) by Milton Bradley.

- *Guess Who* (ages 5+) by Milton Bradley.

- *Mastermind* (ages 8+) or *Mastermind Junior* (ages 5+) by Pavilion.

- *Risk* (ages 10+) by Parker Brothers.

- *30 Second Mysteries* (ages 12+) by University Games.

Vocabulary skills can be practiced with:

- *Boggle* (ages 8+) by Parker Brothers.

- *Password* (ages 8+) by Endless Games.

- *Scrabble* (ages 8+) by Milton Bradley.

The following games by Parker Brothers provide practice with **math skills** for ages 8 and up:

- *Payday*

- *Monopoly*

- *Racko*

☑ Field trips.

Having seen a tiger in the zoo increases a child's understanding when listening to a story about people living in the midst of wild tigers. Seeing a painting, especially its actual size, is even better than looking at a photograph of the artwork.

Incorporate frequent field trips into your schedule. Tour places of business such as a post office, fire station, dairy farm, bread factory, automobile plant, etc. Go to museums of natural history, science, and art. Attend plays, operas, musicals, concerts, historical reenactments, sporting events, and so on.

Watch for day and overnight specialty camps—music, foreign language, science, and art, as well as those offering more traditional camping experiences.

Preparation: Students will gain more from an experience if they have heard or read some background information first and are given specific things to look for or questions to find answers to. This will help direct their thinking during the experience.

Follow-up: Use discussion, composition, a speech, presentation, or an imitation (put on a play, make a display) as a follow-up to field trips. Allow students time to find answers to questions that were raised during the experience. Use resources on hand, or take a trip to the library. Then, allot time for everyone to share discoveries.

☑ Watching videos.

Think of videos as field trips when making selections. Narration along with the sense of "being there" combine to help children better understand a concept. Videos are especially help-ful in situations where a field trip isn't possible—watching a volcano erupt, exotic or dangerous animals in their natural habitats, historical fiction that recreates daily life in a past culture, and so forth.

☑ Making a speech.

Encourage students to make presentations of their research. Keep in mind that research may be as simple as finding pictures of how people dressed in ancient Rome, or explaining the process involved in making silk. Require students to have some sort of illustration for the audience to look at while they speak. Allow a variety of alternatives here—holding up pictures in a book, making models or posters, dressing up in costume, and so on.

☑ Dramatizing a story or idea,
impromptu or prepared.

Young children need to see and experience in order to understand. Before telling my Sunday school class about the parting of the Red Sea, I challenged these four to six-year-olds to separate (part) the water in a cake pan, leaving a dry path, by using only their hands. Each one rushed to take his turn, trying all kinds of maneuvers with his hands before giving up. Next, they cooperated and tried to make walls with all of their hands at once. Finally, they all agreed that it just couldn't be done. Then I told them the story. Their awe was genuine.

During a unit study of ancient Egypt, my seven-year-old son had trouble understanding the idea of flooding. He wondered how the water "knew" when to stop, among other things. I sent him to the sandbox to dig his own "Nile" and flood it with a garden hose. He not only enjoyed the digging, he was thrilled to watch the flooding. He rushed inside, flushed and excited, explaining everything that had baffled him only minutes earlier.

9. Choose activities to teach or practice concepts or skills that suit your children's interests and your budget.

Activities serve one of two purposes—to whet the appetites of students so that they will be motivated to learn the topic, concept, or skill being introduced, or to provide the follow-up necessary for students to absorb the lesson. Suggestions available in curriculum materials should never be considered mandatory. If the student dislikes the activity, neither purpose listed above is likely to be achieved.

Remember that information can be learned, concepts understood, and skills developed in a variety of ways. Don't think of enjoyable activities such as those listed in #4 as something to do if there is time after completing every page in a traditional curriculum package. Instead, look at the objectives and decide the best way to achieve them. Many enjoyable activities can replace work the student finds tedious.

10. Let students have access to answer keys to correct their own daily work.

Emphasize mastery instead of grades. Students should correct any wrong answers. This can be done verbally. Also ask him, or point out, why he made the mistake—lack of attention to detail, not really understanding the question, or not remembering the information, for example. Even if you check the work for young children that find using an answer key tedious, take them through this process. Awareness of the reason behind an error helps you as the teacher to target weak areas, and serves as a model to the student. Eventually, as students realize that **answer keys are to be used to test their understanding**, not just to assign a grade, they will check themselves, correct errors, and think through their mistakes without being told.

Keep Your Perspective

11. Maintain skills, but don't feel compelled to cover every subject every day.

Skills that require rote memory should be taught and maintained by daily practice, including drills, even if the amount of time spent each day varies. It is more effective to schedule breaks—practicing daily for several weeks and then taking one or two weeks off, for example—than to practice now and then.

Concepts can be taught by spending as much time as necessary for a student to grasp them. Follow-up practice can take a variety of forms, including discussion. So, you may find that every subject is not covered every day. I rarely covered both history and science every day since these were subjects supplemented with a number of activities. Frequently, I chose a topic in history and spent one or two weeks with it as a focus, and then spent the next one or two weeks on a topic in science.

12. Have a general back-up plan to handle the unexpected.

When you are too sick to teach or simply must focus your attention on something other than school, young children can still be occupied with worthwhile activities if you keep the following on hand:

- Games.

- Puzzles.

- Art kits or activities with simple instructions.

- Educational videos—purchased or taped from television—labeled and stored especially for such emergencies.

13. Remind yourself of each child's strengths.

It is easy to become so focused on a problem area, whether it is a subject or behavior, that you forget the child has any strengths or talents at all. Provide opportunities for each child to develop in areas where he can succeed with natural ability and perseverance. Not only will he gain self-confidence, but he will also be preparing for his future. After all, we don't choose a career based on our weakest subject!

Regularly reflect on the good qualities of each child. Remember each considerate action or good-hearted motive. Remind yourself that you are shaping each child, which requires time. Above all, realize that your words and actions serve as a model. How they will face obstacles later in life depends on your guidance now.

Make Plans to Suit Multi-levels

The following suggestion is just one of many approaches to teaching several children working at different grade levels.

Divide a planning page into three columns with the headings *Subjects*, *Names*, and *Resources*.

Column 1: List all the subjects you will cover during the school year. Some possibilities are listed below:

Reading Readiness	Spelling
Reading – Phonics	Vocabulary
Reading – Literature	Handwriting
Reading Comprehension	Typing
Composition	Health
Grammar	Science
History	Art
Bible history	Art history

Government   Music appreciation
Geography   Music theory
Physical Education   Bible - Devotions

List subtopics or objectives under the subject. Whenever possible, choose those that several children can work on. For example, first aid would be a subtopic in science and understanding main idea would be an objective in reading comprehension. All students could study both, but using materials appropriate to their own level.

Column 2: Next to each subtopic or subject write the name or initials of each child that will be studying it.

Column 3: Next to the names, list any books, games, field trips, software, or other resources you want to use in that subject with those children. Activities can be written out in order to be an easy reference for gathering materials or as a reminder of what has been done when planning in the future. Otherwise, simply write the title and page numbers of the resource to be used. Note any connections between subjects. For example, a composition topic regarding a famous scientist or inventor might be followed by *"science"* (and possibly *health*) because it connects to that subject.

Outside activities can usually be assigned to a subject area, but any that don't fit can be listed as an additional subject in order to provide a complete profile of each child's work load.

The outline does not have to cover the entire year; it can be expanded as you go. Because it is a working plan, you will add to and subtract from it as need and experience dictates. Allow yourself room to go on tangents rather than feeling bound to the plan, then add it to the list in order to have an accurate record of work accomplished.

Composing your outline on a computer makes it easy to delete anything planned but not done and to add new ideas and resources at any time. By the end of the year you will have a permanent record with a minimum of effort. (Make sure to print out a file copy.)

Detailed objectives covered can be checked off within the Design-A-Study books, or on the charts included in some of these guides by using the student's initials and the date instead of a check mark. This also make future planning easier, since you can see at a glance what has been covered (and when) and what still needs to be included in future plans.

Approaches to record keeping and planning are numerous and varied. At the very minimum, it is helpful in the long run to maintain lists of books read, videos watched, field trips taken, any classes taken outside the home (e.g., music lessons, sports activities, occupational or speech therapy) and their frequency and duration (e.g., twice weekly for three months), along with the titles of resources used in each subject area. Samples of compositions should be kept each year in order to target future objectives in that area based on each child's work.

High School: Record keeping differs at this level. Each student needs an individual record which lists each subject, the number of hours spent in that subject, titles of all resources used, all assigned activities, tests and scores, and final grades. Outside activities should be listed with dates of participation and total hours. This information will then be used to put together a transcript and a resume or a portfolio. The hours will be used to determine whether the subject is one credit (180 hours per credit) or less. The activities and/or test scores can be used to determine a grade.

Records must be kept, but finding the method that works best for your own situation often requires experimentation.

BASIC TEACHING TECHNIQUES

Children who attend public school often play school by assigning work to their dolls or playmates and then standing imperiously over their "students." If this is how you remember imitating teachers as a child, try not to do so as an adult!

Instead, think about a craftsman training an apprentice. Ideally, he encourages, instructs, and guides the student until he is satisfied that his pupil can produce excellent work on his own. The craftsman teaches all skills and concepts necessary to this end and takes pride in handing down his craft.

The end results of our teaching should be young people with a love of learning who are capable of:

☑ Learning independently.

☑ Thinking critically.

☑ Writing clearly, concisely, and convincingly.

☑ Earning a living.

☑ Managing a home.

☑ Raising children.

I also included preparing my children to be servants of God. I wanted them each to have a personal relationship with our Lord and a desire to study the Bible and fulfill God's purpose in their lives.

If you share any of these goals, the following techniques will help you achieve them:

Setting the Tone

Treat all children with respect.

Be fair, firm, gentle-tongued, and polite, expecting the children to imitate you. "Do what I say, not what I do," is *not* an effective approach.

Body language often conveys respect more than words do. Look directly at children and really listen to what they say. React to their comments. Children feel respected if they are listened to even more than if you agree with them.

Be fair and consistent.

If you make a rule, follow through. If you need to change a rule or its consequences, make sure each student is aware of that change. Children become more responsible when they see their world as orderly—a place where behavior has consequences, good and bad.

Praise very specific achievements or behavior.

A general "That's good" is less motivating and instructive than the specific "Your letters slant very evenly, good job!" Making eye contact with a child and saying, "I appreciate how quiet you've been as I've told the story," will not only reinforce that child's good behavior, but encourage the other children to listen quietly as well.

Children sense insincerity, and are suspicious of constant general praise. However, offering regular, sincere, and specific praise will promote a legitimate sense of self-respect.

Remember that every student wants to do well.

Instead of becoming frustrated and demanding when a student complains, refuses, or argues, stop and think about why he might be reacting that way. Then, proceed to solve the problem appropriately. Refer to the section "Problems and Solutions."

Start each day fresh.

Don't begin the day by remembering past frustrations. Our subconscious expectations can affect our facial expressions, eye contact, body language, and voice tone, sending negative signals that encourage the very behavior we hope to change.

Give yourself permission to enjoy learning along with the students.

Hearts and minds open to receive knowledge and wisdom in response to the presence of love and joy. If, instead, you are impatient, frustrated, and perceived as a judge demanding "right" answers, the children will react to situations they find difficult by crying or becoming nervous, sassy, or withdrawn, depending on their personalities.

When you enjoy learning along with the children, you are more likely to be interesting. That alone can prevent many discipline problems.

Formulating the Plan

Choose or adapt materials and activities to suit the student instead of trying to make the student fit the materials.

Remember that materials should be servants, not masters. If tests indicate that the student has accomplished an objective, don't force him to continue to practice simply to complete a workbook or package. For those objectives that do require practice, choose resources and approaches that are best suited for each child.

- If a student has trouble comprehending what he reads, but remembers what he hears, build phonic and reading comprehension skills with short, frequent, specific practice periods, and instruct him in all other areas according to his strength—hearing. Tell him directions or instructions; read questions and allow him to respond orally instead of in writing; read aloud stories and information in other subjects; or use videos, cassettes, and software that speak to the child for you.

- If a student needs to touch (manipulate materials) in order to understand, teach using manipulatives in math and through frequent use of hands-on projects in other subjects. Follow up initial instructions with activities that allow the student to apply the concepts rather than with regular written tests. Recognize that you will both become frustrated by expecting the student to work independently by reading the text and filling in worksheets. Therefore, while the suggestions above may seem like too much work— they will ultimately help the student understand and retain lessons, feel capable of learning, and become confident in his own ability to learn. Independence can be gained gradually, but without this kind of intervention, these students often drop out of school feeling "stupid," unhappy with themselves, and purposeless.

- When a suggested activity would either bore the student, or be too difficult, substitute an activity that meets the same objective, but will be of interest or provide a challenge that is attainable.

Plan short, frequent periods of practice for anything that requires long-term retention.

Typically, phonic skills, spelling, typing, math facts, math skills (that have been mastered but should be kept polished) and memorization of poems, scripts, scriptures, or music to be performed fall into this category.

Cover several subjects or skills at the same time whenever it can be done without causing confusion.

This will allow you to cover much more ground academically. It also helps prevent children from becoming bored.

For instance, if proper handwriting is the objective, and a child is also expected to memorize a poem or scripture, have him write that poem or verse for his handwriting assignment. The words go through his mind as he writes, giving him one of those short, frequent practices, but he can still focus on proper letter formation. This works for the daily practice of spelling words as well.

While my children drew, colored, or cut out pictures for our history timeline, we would sometimes cover objectives in other subjects. They might copy a figure for detail to illustrate costumes of a period as an art lesson, draw a map of the area being studied to reinforce geography skills, or listen to music of the period.

Combining objectives accomplishes two things: it allows you to cover more ground in an interesting way, and helps children maintain attention—which ultimately increases their knowledge and understanding of a subject.

Periodically review progress.

If little or no progress is being made in some area, or the student complains or puts out little effort, consider the following:

- *Are the materials moving at a pace that is too fast? Too slow?* If too fast, stop and supplement with other materials and activities. If too slow, don't assign practice of anything already mastered except for occasional review.

- *Are the materials too difficult for the student to understand without help?* If you want the student to work with materials fairly independently, find another resource. Otherwise, teach the material in your own words through discussion, continuing to assign the problems or discuss the questions. In other words, teach from the materials, but consider them yours, not the student's.

- *Have there been distractions during school hours that may have interfered with the student's ability to concentrate?* What distracts one child may not cause a problem for another. Many students have difficulty focusing on paper/pencil work, or listening to a speaker if there are even slight distractions. Sometimes a student requires a fairly bare work area (or a three-sided divider at his desk to limit his area of visibility) as well as a quiet one. If distractions are a problem, adjust the classroom area so that other children can't intrude, but the teacher can check on progress and help the student focus as necessary. Assign difficult work to be done during the quietest part of the day—other children napping, working quietly out of sight, or attending classes away from home.

Directing the Students

<u>Always</u> be specific about what you expect.

Ask yourself these two questions, "Why am I doing this?" and, "Does the student understand exactly what I consider acceptable?"

Generalities are confusing and overwhelming. Any task is usually made up of several steps. Isolate each step so that the child experiences several small successes by the time he has learned how to carry out the entire task.

For example, the simple task of brushing his own teeth would be modeled one step at a time with the child imitating each step. Gently correct any improper motions, and always smile and/or verbally praise anything done correctly. Use this same technique in academic areas.

Have students hunt for information to share.

There are several benefits to having a child look for answers to questions and then present his information to others:

- Information will be retained longer if it is gathered in order to teach someone else rather than memorized merely to pass a test.

- He sees his work as a contribution instead of a task to win the teacher's approval.

- He becomes part of a team, instead of competing for the teacher's favor.

- He can become excited by the knowledge he is discovering because he is not nervous about memorizing it for a test. You are likely to overhear him telling his friends what he has learned long after that lesson has been completed (self-review).

Don't be quick to supply answers. Instead, ask yourself, "What can I ask the students so that they will come to these conclusions themselves?"

This is basic to the discovery approach to learning. When we gain an insight through our own thinking process rather than just being told, it sticks. Therefore, it is important for the teacher to direct a child's thinking by asking questions. Many math and science materials include this approach.

Replace dry lectures and tedious questions based on your answer key with discussion.

You can tell children what to think, but it is knowing **how** to think that will protect them from the confusing messages that will bombard them once they are off to college or a job. Use discussions to direct students in their thinking. This will serve as a model for them to eventually think critically on their own.

Ask open-ended questions that allow students several answers. Otherwise, it is likely that the students will try to second-guess you in order to "be right" or to please you. This is not thinking. Asking, *"Why...?, What if...?, or How...?"* will direct them to consider and analyze information—thinking critically and creatively. Don't rush in with your opinion. Give them time to think, continuing to ask more narrow questions if they are having difficulty responding or only offer something vague.

For example, if asked what they thought of a movie or book, the vague response, "I didn't like it," would be followed by narrower, more specific questions from you to direct them toward supporting that opinion. If they liked the characters but not the plot you might ask, "Didn't you think the plot was believable?" or "Did you dislike the way the plot was resolved?" Then respond to their answers with your reasoned opinions. It is not a matter of eventually coming to an agreement, but of leading them in the reasoning process. As they become more familiar with the elements of literature and film, they could agree with a movie critic that the plot of a movie was tight, character development consistent and complete, and filming techniques effective, but because they disagree with the moral message, they would not recommend the movie as the critic does.

Use questions in teacher's guides that require students to make inferences, not just those that require recall of facts. Textbooks often include one or two chapter questions labeled "To Think About." Use these for discussions. The Design-A-Study subject books include teaching tips and questions, or statements that can be used as questions, to help you with this technique. *Critical Conditioning* and *Guides to History Plus* include questions for discussion that will aid you in this training process.

You can also supplement discussions with resources that provide students with practice in deductive reasoning. *Mindbenders* are workbooks children usually enjoy while developing this skill. (Available from Critical Thinking Books & Software. Phone 1-800-458-4849 for a catalog or check their website: www.criticalthinking.com.)

Keep your goals in sight.

Most subjects involve several skills and objectives. Therefore, it is necessary for the teacher to target an objective and then remove any unnecessary obstacles. One of the most frequent obstacles to developing various skills in composition is handwriting. Writing (composition) and handwriting are two different subjects. Many young children find handwriting so tiring that instead of allowing themselves to enjoy composing, their minds are filled with a single thought, "How short can I make this and not have to do it again?" Letting them dictate their ideas to you or into a tape recorder can free them to focus on the actual goals. If you also add typing lessons to their schedule, you will be giving them a skill that will make composing and editing easier in the future (once they have developed sufficient speed to type their thoughts). They are also likely to feel more satisfied by the neat results.

Change direction whenever your plans aren't working.

Don't be a slave to a method or to the idea of completion. If a lesson or activity doesn't work out, either make adjustments, or don't waste any more time on it.

If a student finds an assigned book to be boring or too difficult to understand, decide whether or not it is a book he should finish. If so, read it aloud to him in order to offer explanations of anything he may find confusing, rather than demanding that he continue on his own.

A book may seem boring when the problem is actually the student's inability to comprehend it. He is unable to create a mental picture as he reads. This could be caused by an inability to read quickly or fluently enough, by a lack of vocabulary skills, or because he does not have the background to understand the life experiences in the story. Discussing the story as you read it to the student can help him appreciate what he cannot understand on his own.

On the other hand, there are times when you may decide not to have the student continue with an assignment. You may discover that a workbook you thought would take several weeks to complete only has a few useful pages because the student understands the objectives quickly. In that case, don't force him to complete every page just because you hate to see the pages "wasted."

WHAT TO EXPECT

A general idea of what is considered typical behavior at various ages can be helpful in planning lessons.

PRESCHOOL: AGES 2 - 4

Boisterous and noisy, preschoolers need to move. Their fingers aren't coordinated enough for writing or cutting. Coloring will be mostly scribbles. They learn through seeing, hearing, and touching, by asking "why," or "how," by imitation, and by repetition, which they enjoy.

Age 2

Unpredictable, two-year-olds can go from kissing to hitting in a moment. They dawdle, act on impulse, and imitate what they have seen. Choices are difficult. Direct instructions work best. They are content to play alone, but near others. A firm, but gentle, voice explaining why, while physically directing or stopping behavior, will have better results than shouting. This also provides the kind of model you want them to imitate.

Age 3

More social, the three-year-old may want to feel a part of family activities. Because his attention span is still very short, he can be quite satisfied with a small task as long as you sound the same as when you direct the others (so he feels it is as important).

Age 4

Non-stop chatter that mixes fantasy with reality is perhaps the best description of this age. Full of energy, they must have activities to keep them busy, or they are likely to fight over toys, wrestle, practice jungle noises, or otherwise become a major distraction. Your verbal commands may work momentarily, but physical intervention remains the best way to direct their behavior. By physical intervention I mean using touch to control a child, whether it means grabbing his hand to prevent him from rushing into the street, or keeping him by your side with an arm around him to prevent his wandering during lessons. Sometimes, simply physically moving a child from one place to another can keep things running smoothly.

Generally, four-year-olds want to please and respond to praise (for a few minutes, anyway). It will be much easier to plan a variety of simple activities than to become a drill sergeant. They love to listen to and then act out stories, play house, move to music, play with sand, water, and clay, climb, and practice hopping, jumping and other movements.

PRIMARY:
AGES 5 - 7

From five to seven you will see a progression toward greater ability to work calmly and quietly. But, even though children are becoming more ready and able for fine motor tasks such as drawing, writing, and cutting, their hands still become quite tired. Their tension is often expressed by making noises while they work, or sticking out their tongues as they concentrate.

The bulk of the day should be more experience-oriented. All children at this age should have materials to touch, handle, and explore. Their interest in any activity makes a big difference in how long they will pay attention (up to 20 minutes), so a project approach to learning will be the most successful.

Eager to learn, these children often plunge into a new activity. Just as easily, however, they can become discouraged and quit. Their bodies don't seem to allow them to do the perfect work their minds imagine. Offer patient encouragement. Explain that we all have trouble sometimes, and that you only expect their best. Do this in a matter-of-fact manner, since too much coaxing often makes them self-conscious.

This is also a competitive age, so you are likely to hear a lot of boasting. Since they want approval, they can be motivated by praise from an adult. It is essential, however, that the adult not attempt to motivate the child by comparing his behavior to that of another child—

61

"Why can't you be good like Janie?" This breeds resentment. Instead, praise "Janie" directly and specifically. The disobedient child will often quickly change his behavior to be praised just like "Janie."

Incorporate opportunities for movement into lesson plans. Children in this age range continue to express themselves physically and enjoy learning when movement is involved.

They want to find out why, but still think in very concrete terms. Therefore, use field trips, videos, and books with illustrations to help them learn about their world—how water gets into their faucets, how food gets to their grocery store, or why they must brush their teeth, for example.

Encourage budding reasoning skills with jokes, riddles, and puns. Strengthen memory skills by having children play games in which they must recall the position of an item, or name up to five items that were displayed and then covered. Encourage them to memorize songs, including those that will help them later, such as the ABC song, addition facts, or scriptures set to music.

You will usually notice a big difference from ages five to seven in both coordination necessary for handwriting (fine motor control) and in attention span. This is why many educators advise waiting to teach reading and writing until age seven or eight.

Teach according to the readiness of the child. Some are eager to learn to read, despite their lack of coordination. Let them learn, even if you only teach two minutes at a time. But don't rush the others.

INTERMEDIATE:
AGES 8 - 10

Physical coordination improves greatly during this period. Children can also handle group situations such as games and sports more easily. However, boys remain more physically oriented and boisterous than girls, and continue to need more of an outlet for their energy. Girls frequently do well at the fine motor (paper and pencil) tasks, and are generally more capable of sitting longer than boys to work at quiet tasks. They may even complain that boys are too loud or too rough.

The longer attention span and ability to practice repetitive tasks (i.e., more willing to persevere) makes children in this age range easier to teach than younger children. But, most still need to have a change of pace after 15 or 20 minutes, even if it's only a new approach to the same subject matter. That time may increase if the children are keenly interested in a task or activity. However, they continue to lose interest fairly quickly, in general, and still need regular change in focus or activities to maintain attention.

Children this age enjoy expressing their opinions to gain a sense of authority. They respond well to presenting information to others. Give them plenty of opportunity to shine.

JUNIOR:
AGES 11-12

These years set the stage for the teens and can be filled with mood swings. Children at this age may overreact to stress. They are especially concerned with things being "fair."

Thinking begins to become more abstract. They are able to use logic to solve problems, and form an hypothesis to test. This is the age to focus on the development of critical thinking skills. However, continue to include concrete experiences, not just explanations, to increase understanding of new concepts.

Although now able to concentrate for a longer period of time, these children still need shifts in activities from quiet to active.

JUNIOR HIGH:
AGES 13 - 15

Emotions may continue to be on a roller coaster ride, causing kids this age to overreact to stress. The opinions of friends carry more weight than ever and fitting in becomes very important. They want <u>and</u> <u>need</u> to discuss issues; to have their opinions heard.

These children are capable of working independently, thinking critically, and reasoning abstractly to a much greater degree than at younger ages. However, concepts are still more easily understood if they are part of the student's experience.

SENIOR HIGH:
AGES 16 - 18

Emotionally, children at this age both want and fear independence and the world of dating, driving, and work. They tend to want to change the world, and are often zealous, working hard for causes they believe in. Give them outlets— writing letters to congressmen or to an editor, witnessing, and carrying pro-life signs at rallies. They need to "make a difference."

They are now capable of abstract thinking to solve problems and understand concepts, and wrestle with questions of faith, wanting to find answers for themselves. Capable of independent learning to a great degree, they should be developing good study skills or habits and the ability to search out answers. Give them more control over their own learning.

LEARNING STYLES

Age influences coordination, ability to reason, attention span, and emotions. However, learning style and personality separate children within the same age group. There are numerous books available which offer a variety of learning categories and labels. The following is just one of many acceptable approaches to gaining insight into how each child learns.

Anything we find confusing or complicated is best learned when we can see, hear, <u>and</u> do something in order to understand it. In general, by age 8 or 9, a person is stronger in one of those three areas: seeing (the visual learner), hearing (the auditory learner), or doing (the kinesthetic, or hands-on learner). However, children may also continue to exhibit a combination of styles. Become familiar with each style, but use observation and conversation with the child to help you in choosing teaching methods and materials. Sometimes, all it takes for a child to understand the lesson is a change in how the information is presented.

The **visual learner** prefers to look at illustrations or text, or to watch others do something, rather than listen only. He tends to remember what he has seen. (This child may be able to tell you where you left your keys.) As an adult, he or she is likely to be a note-taker and list-maker. The traditional approach, textbooks, and workbooks are comfortable to this type of learner.

The **auditory learner** prefers listening. Therefore, he prefers discussions and audiocassettes—especially anything put to music—to reading texts and filling in workbooks. He may annoy the teacher by not looking at her when she speaks, and yet, he is often able to parrot back exactly what was just said. He seems to memorize easily what he hears. Sociable, often a chatterbox who enjoys trying to be funny, he wants to be the center of attention, and is likely to favor group projects, discussions, presentations, and videos to the traditional textbook approach. Weak areas may be a sense of time (we think he dawdles; he disagrees) handwriting, following written directions, and organizational skills.

The **kinesthetic learner** needs to do, not just watch or listen, to gain understanding. He tends to prefer field trips (or, at least, videos that show real places and people while explanations are narrated), projects, and computer software that allows him to become directly involved in the lesson.

Choose the approach to instruction, activities for practice, and projects for application of knowledge that suit your children's best avenue of learning.

How Does Personality Affect Learning?

Perhaps the most obvious example is the child that is forever getting into trouble. He—boys outnumber girls in this situation—needs to touch and move. This impulse is stronger than the desire to please. Even though he wants to obey, he may not. If you try to sit him down with a text and a workbook, he may either cry, quit, or simply refuse to work. A great deal of frustration on both sides can be avoided simply by allowing him to manipulate objects, build or make something, or experiment and explore for the bulk of his learning.

Some children prefer a quiet, orderly routine and actually want to read and write. They like the sense of accomplishment they feel when checking off a task completed, or counting the number of problems done correctly. They make lists and finish homework. Adult approval is very motivating, so you aren't likely to have many discipline problems. In fact, they are often annoyed by those impulsive types.

At first you may be lulled into thinking that this must be the ideal student. You could ask "him," although it's even more likely to be a her, to read the text and fill out the workbook pages while you get to those thousand-and-one other things demanding your attention. But, he is not necessarily working from a desire to learn or know. Rather, achievement or approval provides a sense of satisfaction. Therefore, long-term retention may be a problem.

These students may get good grades in public schools since the curriculum appears orderly and they may be motivated by grades. However, high grades can usually be achieved by students who carry out instructions, turn in work on time, and test well due to the ability to recall information. Critical thinking skills may fall by the wayside. Therefore, these "ideal" students may still be prey to the influence of others in positions of authority—professors and assigned readings, for example. Prepare these children by encouraging them to experiment, examine, find answers, disagree, and prove their opinions.

Some children just want to know. That desire is greater than wanting to touch, achieve, or please. Any topic that grabs their attention will pull them into a study of great depth and detail. These are the true learners that often drop out of the traditional school setting. You'll find many examples in biographies of famous men and women. Accounts reveal that they read voraciously and/or experimented repeatedly, persevering and learning mostly on their own, or under the guidance of a knowledgeable mentor. Help these children develop skills that will aid them in studies that they want to pursue. Choose formats the students find appealing or explain how the lesson is necessary for them to accomplish something else that they already desire to understand in order to maintain their attention and cooperation.

Certainly there are other personality factors that enter into learning styles. Some children forever ask why they need to know something. They are practical and want to make sense of things. They may learn best by doing, or want the orderliness of routine, or prefer to follow their interests and dig deeply into a subject, but first they must see that the information has some value to them.

The traditional approach to learning satisfies only one type of learner—the visual, orderly student. And then, it does not necessarily help him to become a critical thinker. An eclectic approach—the use of unit studies, projects, and/or varied resources chosen to suit the needs of the each student—allows the teacher to remain focused on reaching children at every developmental stage, no matter what their learning style and despite teaching several children with different needs at the same time.

Teaching Tips for the Visual Learner

1. Use visual aids: pictures, charts, and graphs.

2. Provide an orderly learning area. These learners tend to be more productive when surroundings are neat.

3. Use color as a visual aid if a student has difficulty learning to read or spell a word. Color over the troublesome portion with a yellow or orange highlighter, or write that portion of the word in red or orange.

4. Include activities that allow the student to make a visual record of information—copy key ideas, take notes, record information on charts or graphs, make time lines, etc.

5. Include written drills, not just recitation of facts to be memorized.

Teaching Tips for the Auditory Learner

1. Tell the student what to do rather than have him read directions. Look for specific practice materials that will appeal to the student in order to build skill in following written directions without letting that weakness interfere with other learning.

2. Let the student tell you answers, using discussion instead of always requiring written answers on workbook pages.

3. Read aloud or use books on tape and videos to broaden his base of literature, following up with comprehension questions for discussion.

4. Allow the student to read out loud when by himself. This often increases the speed of comprehending what is being read.

5. Allow the student to talk out loud to himself about whatever he is trying to retain. Teach him this technique as a study skill.

6. Explain steps clearly when teaching a task that requires organization. The student will need an outline to follow or a list of steps for reference. Remind him patiently as needed while he develops skills in this area.

7. Provide a quiet place to work since sound becomes a distraction.

Teaching Tips for the Kinesthetic Learner

1. Use manipulatives.

2. Teach through activities that allow the student to move and explore.

3. Use a reading program that allows the student to learn by using all the senses: see-hear-do.

4. Allow the student to read out loud or talk to himself (think out loud) when he works independently.

DISCIPLINE

There are numerous books available about raising children that include discipline. This list simply highlights a few basic ideas that every teacher should know.

Be consistent.

This is the very heart of successful discipline. Children will test you—you can absolutely count on that. Despite their protests, they actually feel secure when they find boundaries, so "plug your ears" (ignore emotional appeals) and carry out any reasonable consequences you have threatened.

Be fair.

Because consistency is essential, threats must never be idle or exaggerated. Consequences should be appropriate to the behavior so that behavior will change. If every wrong is met with a spanking, you are likely to face a rebellious child. But, if spanking is reserved for deliberate disobedience (rebellion), it will be more likely that the child will become obedient.

The consequence for making a mess should be cleaning it up. If a child hits or fights, he may need to sit in a chair for a few minutes, separated from the group, in order to compose himself. This is often referred to as "Time Out." An overly energetic child that can't seem to pay attention may need to run a few laps around the yard until he's tired enough to sit still.

Be reasonable.

Don't expect more than a child is capable of doing. A two-year-old may answer you with, "No, no, no," just because he's two. You can laugh, say "Yes, yes, yes," and physically carry out whatever must be done, or distract him from whatever he is getting into. Likewise, a toddler that knows no fear may need a harness when you go out so that he doesn't run off into danger.

Be willing to change your mind if you think the consequences would not be appropriate. For example, say, "I told you that if you did that you would have to ___, but since you did ___" or, "since then I realized ___" or, simply, "but, I've changed my mind," and explain the new consequences. This isn't perceived as inconsistency, but as justice or mercy, depending on the situation—unless you do it all the time and simply appear wishy-washy.

At three, my daughter was a strong-willed child, constantly testing limits. One day someone broke a glass at the bottom of the stairs. I told her not to go down, explaining that the broken glass could cut her bare feet. Only minutes later I heard her at the bottom of the steps! When she saw my angry expression, she quickly pointed to the boots she had slipped into before descending. "See, Mommy, I won't get cut." Being reasonable meant not punishing her—she had acted as a problem solver. To her, my reason for keeping her upstairs had been eliminated and her actions were not disobedient.

Be specific.

Children need to know exactly what is expected. This makes them responsible for their behavior. Get into the habit of explaining why. Rules that make sense to the child are more readily obeyed.

If you appear to be an authority that passes out punishments on a whim, children see themselves as innocent victims. Then you face growing resentment instead of changing behavior.

Don't be afraid to change the rules or the consequences.

The children need to be aware of the change, of course, but change itself doesn't cause a problem. Sometimes a consequence, whether a reward or a punishment, becomes ineffective and must be changed. At other times, you might make adjustments because the children are more mature. For example, when my children were young and careless, they were required to eat only at the kitchen table. Occasionally, they were granted permission to eat while watching television if they promised to clean up after themselves. Leaving a mess meant a return to the "table only" rule for a while. Eventually, they proved to be responsible in this area and there was no further need of a rule. They were treated like any adult.

Don't yell.

Discipline is much more effective if it is carried out matter-of-factly. Don't allow children to draw you into debates and discussions. Ignore their attempts at emotional blackmail and stand firm. Otherwise you may be drawn into a shouting match. Remember that you do not need to convince them that you are right.

*   *   *

Following these rules may not be easy. There will probably be periods that the children seem to get the best of you. But keep these goals in sight. The more you follow them, the sooner you will see positive results. And the more consistent you are when children are young, the fewer problems you will have when they reach their teens.

Balance Discipline With These Confidence Boosters

How we interact with children affects their self-confidence and their later desire to persevere when faced with challenges. Discipline should take place within an encouraging atmosphere—one that can easily be created and maintained with a minimum of effort:

Sincerely and specifically praise each child for his effort.

The confidence he feels motivates him to continue trying. When only major achievements or successes are praised, a child may eventually quit working toward something as soon as he believes he will not be the best, or cannot reach some standard of perfection, or because he believes he will never be able to please you.

"Catch" your child when he behaves well.

A word of praise will not only build confidence, but will also encourage him to behave correctly at other times.

Listen.

Take time to listen to whatever is on your child's mind. You don't have to stop working, just respond in a manner that assures him your mind is with him even though you are doing chores. Responses should be respectful. If he has expressed opinions you want to disagree with, do it as if he is an adult. That is, avoid stern-sounding lectures and respond with support for your opposing views. The sense of being heard, not agreed with, is what provides a sense of confidence.

Provide plenty of opportunities for the child to make discoveries.

This is a sure way for a child to feel smart, and that's always a confidence booster! The easiest way to do this is to occasionally direct children to find answers instead of automatically supplying them. For example, when I was five I noticed that my playmate's sandbox had soft white sand unlike the coarse brown grains piled in my yard. I asked my mother what sand was made of. Instead of telling me, she handed me several sifters and said, "Why don't you see if you can find out?" Eagerly I sifted the sand and studied the results. I rushed in to announce my brilliant discovery, "It's made of little stones!" Wisely she responded with a smile. It never occurred to me that she already knew; I thought I was teaching her, and I felt wonderful.

Always treat your children with the same polite respect you want them to show to you and others.

How we are treated affects our sense of confidence. If we are called names, and/or rarely praised, we feel less capable in *every* situation we face, not just situations similar to our negative experiences.

Freely, and regularly, tell each child you love him.

Children want and need the love of their parents. Don't assume that they know you love them. Children frequently misunderstand our behavior. The young feel unloved every time they are disciplined, which is usually quite often. Counter all of this with lots of verbal reminders of your love.

Remind each child of his good qualities.

This is welcome at any time, but is especially important if your child has been experiencing any sort of struggle. It helps balance his perspective and prevents him from feeling defeated or worthless. Remind him of times when he was helpful, kind, patient, generous, carried out chores without complaint, told the truth even when he thought the consequences would be unpleasant, and kept trying something even if he didn't actually succeed. These are all qualities we want to see develop more and more—and that takes encouragement.

PROBLEMS & SOLUTIONS

When faced with a problem, look for the underlying reasons, and then choose the solution accordingly.

Problem   The student has trouble with . . .

Solution

No matter what the area, break it down into manageable parts. Then teach each part or step until the child succeeds before moving on.

If the parts are too difficult, it may simply be a matter of readiness. Set it aside and introduce it weeks or months later.

If the student has had the difficulty beyond the age that most children accomplish the task, readiness is probably not the reason. Now you need to find materials and approaches to use that will allow the information to enter by sight, sound, and touch as much as possible. Practice frequently. Once a day is a minimum. Practice to the point of saturation—the child's eyes glaze and you know that not one drop more will enter his mind—it could be five minutes or fifty. Encourage the student. Try to make everything interesting and pleasant. Remember that all children want to do well.

Problem   The student hates to read.

Solution

Encourage a love of reading by selecting appealing books, or having him select books, and reading out loud to him regularly and frequently. Meanwhile, target the specific comprehension or phonic difficulties that are the underlying problem and, using frequent practice to the saturation point, build skill where there is now weakness.

One way for parents to head off this problem is to read around, not just to, their children. Children, especially young ones, want to be like their parents. If they see their parents reading to themselves often, they will have a much greater desire to learn to read "like Mom and Dad."

Problem   The student hates reading because he is not a visual learner.

Reading may not be the easiest way for the student to understand or remember information. If he has been forced to learn most subjects by reading texts and/or workbooks, a combination of frustration and boredom has probably built up until he is now burned out and rebellious.

Solution

Eliminate reading as the primary path of information by verbally explaining instructions and reading both fiction and nonfiction out loud. Videos and audiocassettes can be used when the teacher is unavailable. Allow the student to answer questions orally. Then, schedule increased practice time to build reading comprehension and phonic skills using materials that incorporate sight, sound, and hands-on activities as much as possible.

Problem   The student hates to read because decoding skills are weak.

If the student frequently hesitates when reading out loud, decoding (phonic) skills are weak.

Solution

Short, frequent practices, including drill, should be scheduled throughout the day. Continue until fluency in reading indicates that his phonic skills are no longer weak.

Begin with a brief review of phonic symbols the student has mastered. Have him say the sound represented, then read a list of words using that sound. For example, "th" followed by the words then, that, bath, bother.

Use any words that the student finds difficult as an opportunity to review any applicable phonic rule or to provide helpful approaches to sounding out entire words. For example, the student might hesitate when he sees "bother" because it has two syllables. Cover the last syllable (er) and have him try again. If he reads the first syllable as the word both, tell him the "o" is short, When he pronounces it correctly, uncover the "er" for him to sound out. Then have him read the entire word again, fluently. Continue with this type of practice.

For persistent problems in retaining words studied, combine the senses: seeing, hearing, and doing. The student should copy the word with his finger in a tray of cornmeal, sand, or on a piece of velvet— anything with a distinct texture—while he says each syllable out loud. This approach is effective in introducing letters and sounds as well, especially with kinesthetic learners. He should also trace the word written on paper with a pencil or marker, and then copy the word (writing it while looking at the model). Some children are able to skip the first two activities and copy the words by writing them, saying the word each time they write it.

Require the student to read daily from readers at both his **independent** and **instructional levels.** Readers are books that contain a controlled vocabulary in order to provide specific practice in conjunction with the phonic rules being introduced. A student being instructed at a second grade level should be able to read first grade readers **independently.** That practice will increase his speed, fluency, and ability to read with expression, as well as provide the student with sense of success and confidence in his ability to read. An easy way to incorporate this practice into the schedule is to have the student read to a younger sibling.

Readers at the student's **instructional level** include many words he can already read, but because they include words currently being taught, these books should be read out loud to the teacher so that he will have help as it is needed.

Print common sight words and various words that the student finds difficult on index cards. Set a timer for one or two minutes several times throughout the day and have the child read as many word cards as he can.

Record the results. Maintaining a record allows the student to see his progress.

Before having the student read a new story, skim it for words that are new or likely to cause difficulty. Have him practice reading each of those words, before starting the story.

Problem	The student hates to read because reading comprehension skills are weak.

Solution

The student should immediately reread any portion that he has read slowly and hesitantly in order to read it more fluently. With all attention focused on sounding out words, he is unlikely to have had a grasp of the meaning of what was read the first time through.

Extra comprehension practice should include reading and carrying out short written instructions for a game, recipe, or project. Choose instructions that the student will find appealing, that uses words he can read easily, and that are simple enough to ensure his success. If he is learning to read from a specific curriculum, choose materials for this assignment from at least one level below that being used for his reading instruction. If the reading program used for instruction is grade three, for example, use activities for following directions from second grade materials.

If the student becomes upset or frustrated and begs you to tell him the instructions, remind him that this lesson is to help him understand what he reads. Suggest that he read it out loud—either to you or to himself. However, if he does not understand the meaning of a word, explain it rather than requiring him to use a dictionary at this point. Once the assignment has been completed, reward him with a lesson that does not involve reading.

Problem   **The student hates to read because he finds the material boring.**

The student may have adequate phonic and comprehension skills for the assigned text, but because he finds the subject or style boring or tedious, his mind wanders while his eyes skim across the words. Rather than a failure to comprehend, this is a failure to read thoughtfully.

Solution

If an assigned reading bores a student, cover your objective using a different story or book. Or, if it is nonfiction information, skim the selection and explain the main points to the student in your own words.

Sometimes students claim boredom because they can't picture what they are reading—it doesn't seem real to them. They may be able to find the dictionary definitions of words, but cannot really picture the strange vocabulary, and aren't drawn in by the author's style. These books can be read out loud to the students. Often hearing it read with expression, and with explanations of unfamiliar words and ideas, makes it enjoyable.

For example, I had assigned a children's version of *The Iliad*, but my daughter, then 12 and an eager reader, just couldn't seem to understand it. The unfamiliar names and setting became a hurdle she couldn't seem to overcome. I read the book out loud and it became a favorite!

Problem   The student hates reading because of the follow-up questions or book reports.

The student may complain about reading assignments not because he dislikes reading, but because he faces what he considers tedious drilling or grilling about the story or book. Or, he may simply dislike composing book reports.

Solution

To remove the barrier the student has built up toward reading, assign a story and then tell him that he won't have to answer lists of questions or write a book report. You would, however, like him to tell you what he likes and doesn't like about the story.

Give him plenty of books with freedom from the past routine before you ask more specific questions. Then only ask a few questions, without an answer key in front of you, so that the student feels free to discuss what was read. Use questions that don't necessarily require you to read the book but do require the student to think about what he has read. *Critical Conditioning,* available from Design-A-Study, includes such questions. You can also use study guides for specific titles as long as you glance at the guide and then enter into a discussion so that the atmosphere remains relaxed.

Teach reading comprehension skills by assigning short selections for that purpose. For example, ask the student to read a specific psalm, then have him tell you the theme, and the meaning of any metaphors. Several companies carry workbooks that focus on specific skills, such as finding the main idea or identifying cause and effect. These types of resources are helpful since the student only has to read one or two paragraphs before answering questions. However, follow-up should include the application of these skills within a larger context.

Students capable of summarizing can be assigned book and movie reviews instead of book reports. These provide a more interesting approach and encourage critical thinking. Allow the auditory or kinesthetic learners, especially, to present their reviews orally if they dislike any assignment requiring handwriting.

Frequently reading out loud to children, encouraging them to read books of their choice, and reserving questions and reports for only some, but not all, assignments, contributes to an overall enjoyment of literature.

Problem	The student hates composition.
Solution	Target the reason (below) and proceed with that remedy.
Problem	The student hates composition because he dislikes handwriting.

If the student writes slowly, assignments take a long time to complete—time he would rather spend doing something fun. If his hand gets tired when he writes—a common complaint among the young—then he will try to avoid any lessons involving handwriting.

Solution

Remove the handwriting aspect from composition. Let the student dictate stories into a tape recorder or to you. Teach him to type. However, don't expect him to type his own work until he has developed sufficient speed.

Problem   The student hates composition
          Because he feels overwhelmed by
          the assignment.

This is especially likely if composition has been taught by using workbook exercises that are followed by occasional, but lengthy, assignments such as reports or research papers. In that case, the student may not be prepared for all that is involved in the assignment. He has learned isolated aspects of writing, but has not had enough practice applying each skill.

Solution

Be very specific about what you want the student to do. Begin with just one skill for the first assignment, ensuring a successful experience. Begin with a narrow topic that the student will find interesting in order to change his opinion about composition assignments.

For example, ask him to write a short description of any object in the room without naming it. He should choose words that will help you, his audience, picture this object in your mind when you read his paragraph. Remind him to think about the object using all of his senses. The description should include size, shape, color, texture, aroma (if any), taste (if any), and use. All of this instruction directs him toward successful development of the skill targeted by this lesson—using a more exact vocabulary in writing.

Comprehensive Composition, available from Design-A-Study, provides a more thorough explanation of teaching skills step-by-step. That and the activity ideas it includes should prove helpful in this situation.

Problem   The student hates composition because he dislikes the assigned topics.

Solution

Since the objective is usually to increase specific composition skills, permit the student a choice of topics or the opportunity to think of one on his own. Also notice the types of assignments that are making him uncomfortable. For example, if he has been required to write creatively, he may feel as if he has run out of ideas. Switch to descriptive, expository, or persuasive writing, or provide a model for imitation. That is, read several entertaining poems by one author, or several tall tales, and ask the student to write one of his own in the same style.

At times you may want to assign a topic that will increase the student's knowledge of specific content while building his writing skill. Wait until he has had a period of choice and then assign a topic that will allow him to use resources he finds appealing in order to gather the information—library books, software, the Internet, and so on.

| Problem | The student hates composition because he feels as if it is all he does. |

If the student has been expected to write each day, either something new or a continuation of a longer assignment, he may just be tired of thinking about writing. This is more likely to be the case if the daily assignments have not been interesting or varied, he has run out of creative ideas, or feels as if his compositions meet too much criticism.

Solution

Children can be expected to work on composition skills daily without becoming overwhelmed. Use the following approaches:

- Incorporate activities and games that build various skills without writing. For example, take turns describing something in the room until the other players guess the object. This builds skill in vocabulary that will be applied later in their descriptive writing. Build skill in resolving problems in their own future stories by stating a problem and asking students for possible solutions.

- Don't require everything they write to be read and corrected by you. Some days let the children write for their own private files. Then, occasionally ask if they want to choose something from that file to work on with you as an assignment to be polished.

- If the students are bored by routine, vary the amount of time allotted for composition. Some days the students may have just enough time to jot down a few ideas. Other days, especially during the final, polishing stage, allow enough time to complete the assignment.

Problem	The student can spell words correctly on a weekly test, but forgets those spellings in his written work.

Solution

First, be certain that the words to be memorized are printed rather than written in cursive, for clarity. Then help the student learn to approach spelling logically, rather than by attempting to memorize a series of letters. Have the student:

- Memorize words in groups of two or more that have a sight-sound pattern in common (e.g., achieve, chief, belief). This aids long-term retention.

- Say each syllable, noticing what letters make up that sound. For any especially hard-to-remember words, have the student highlight the syllable that may be causing difficulty with a bright color such as yellow or orange.

- Build a family of words by adding prefixes and suffixes to the base word of each word on his spelling list whenever possible. E.g., achieve: achieves, achieved, achieving, achievement. Spelling rules are now practiced regularly in a meaningful way—vocabulary is broadened, and the use of a logical approach to spelling is reinforced.

- Practice one-minute drills throughout the day. Print especially troublesome words on index cards (one word per card). The student should read a word, look away and spell it out loud, then check himself. He should continue this procedure with the next card, completing as many as he can in one minute.

Design-A-Study's *Natural Speller,* a complete spelling program for all ages, already organizes words in a sight-sound pattern, provides lists of prefixes and suffixes, and all rules for syllabication and spelling in order to carry out the suggestions listed above.

Problem	The student has a short attention span and is hard to control.
Solution	Target the reason (below) and act accordingly.

The student may be a hands-on learner with an impulsive personality. If this is the case, the teacher may need to continually help the student refocus on a task. One way to do this is to incorporate outlets for his need to "do."

- Adjust lessons to allow more verbal interaction and physical movement. During a lesson about parts of speech, for example, ask him to act out a verb for you to guess, or to touch as many nouns in the room as he can in five seconds.

- Gain the student's attention by asking open-ended questions instead of those requiring only recall of what was heard or read. In other words, encourage him to have an opinion and to gain insight by asking, "What do you think?" or "What would you do?" whenever it is apparent that he is becoming distracted.

- When giving instructions, stop after each step and ask the student to explain whatever you just said in his own words, and, if appropriate, carry out that step.

- Work toward increases in duration of attention as a separate goal using techniques for behavior management. Many books focusing on Attention Deficit Disorder (A.D.D.) contain suggestions that anyone can find useful in dealing with this problem. Check your local library for books that offer practical suggestions for managing behavior, including those concerning A.D.D., or check the materials offered by the companies listed in the next chapter.

The student's behavior could be due to confusion over the lesson.

Some children crumble the moment something doesn't come easily. When instructions or explanations sound unclear or too complicated, they give up. If this is the case, back up, slow down, and change your wording. Separate the skill or objective into small steps that can be accomplished successfully one at a time, using illustrations along with your verbal instructions. Remind the students that it is your job to find a way to help them understand, and it is their job to let you know when they don't so that you can try something different.

The student may be bored.

This can be the result of using resources that don't suit the student's learning style, that he finds dull, or that contain content he finds too easy or too difficult. Over time, the student may become more and more restless, completing little despite having sufficient time for each assignment.

If this has become a regular behavioral problem, you may need to change your approach to teaching. Temporarily provide a break from routine by putting away the books and workbooks and stopping any regular skill practices. Plan a project that you know the student will find interesting. Read stories and nonfiction out loud. Play games. Do experiments. Take nature walks. Make each day fun, letting learning just "sneak in." Then, gradually, include short periods of one-on-one lessons in such skill areas as reading, math, and spelling, increasing the number of sessions before increasing the length of time for any one practice period.

Problem   The student won't cooperate. He doesn't want to do anything.

Once a student no longer cooperates and wants to expend as little energy as possible, it is likely that he has decided that learning is merely a requirement—not something to be enjoyed. Asked to find and present information, this student is likely to complain, preferring to read the text and fill in worksheets because it takes less effort. This is usually the result of an accumulation of experience that led to discouragement, boredom, and/or complacency.

Solution

- Temporarily set aside all expectations and past teaching techniques. Allow the student to absorb content by reading to him, using videos, audio-cassettes, and/or computer software that includes narration. Involve him in discussions rather than having him listen to lectures. Have him experiment to discover a concept rather than simply illustrate one already taught, which he is likely to regard as a waste of time.

- Assign projects that are interesting to the student but will require him to apply a number of skills. He will continue to accomplish objectives, but in a new way. For example, the student could choose a country or area to study (ensuring his interest). If he doesn't like a textbook approach but needs help organizing his work, he can use the question guide in the *Guides to History Plus* as an outline to cover history and geography objectives. He will also be practicing research skills in order to find information. If he writes down that information in response to the questions, he will also be practicing preliminary note-taking skills. This will also allow him greater ease in organizing a final paper than having pages of notes for each source, mixing the categories of information covered. Map skills are covered if he completes a map to indicate the location of the country, and, depending on his age, maps indicating climate or terrain. Various other skills can be involved, depending on his final presentation. He could include illustrations of the country's flag and anything he finds interesting—wildlife, famous figures, buildings, clothing, tools, types of transportation, etc. He could also collect, make, and/or cook items for a display.

- Use techniques to encourage learning by discovery. You will need to prepare and guide the student so that he discovers a concept rather than just telling him (or having him read it) and then requiring him to memorize it. Instead of announcing that green plants need light, for instance, ask the student what he thinks would happen if a plant never had any light. Then help him design an experiment to find out. This can be as simple as placing one plant on a windowsill and an identical plant in a dark closet. The child would give each plant the same amount of water each day, looking for any changes at that time. Those simple observations are the clues he will use to draw the conclusion (discover) that plants need light.

- Since the goal is to direct the student in a manner that will increase his desire to learn for its own sake, be careful to act as an encourager, not a judge. Listen to his complaints and negotiate solutions.

The student needs to experience learning as interesting without, at least at first, exerting any more effort than he has in the past. Once he begins to enjoy learning he will put in more time and effort voluntarily and without complaint.

As he relaxes a bit, begin to schedule time to work on skills that have been temporarily avoided, using resources or techniques he will find appealing (e.g., workbooks, software, one-on-one discussion). If the student has had great difficulty learning basic skills— reading, reading comprehension, writing, and math— look for materials to work in those areas that have been developed for students with special needs even if he has never been diagnosed with a particular problem. These materials will usually be multi-sensory and move more slowly through each step than traditional curriculum materials. (Refer to the list of companies in the next chapter.)

TEACHING CHILDREN WITH SPECIAL NEEDS

Each child is unique, and the obstacles to his learning specific. However, there are general techniques that can be applied to most situations.

Explain instructions verbally.

1. Be certain that you have the child's attention by making eye contact before you explain instructions.

2. Keep directions simple. Use words he will understand, but be concise.

3. Have the student repeat the instructions before beginning a task in order to be certain that they are, indeed, understood.

4. Any tasks that are carried out daily should become part of a routine. Schedule the tasks either at a certain time each day, or as part of an order in which lessons take place. That is, the task always follows and/or precedes the same thing.

5. Patiently repeat instructions as often as necessary, using the same wording each time.

Choose multi-sensory resources.

1. Use materials that involve as many of the senses as possible: seeing, hearing, and touching. Or, adapt materials already on hand. For example, read the word problems in the text out loud to the student, direct his thinking using manipulatives or illustrations as needed, and have him answer either verbally or by writing the equation and its solution.

2. Try audiocassette tapes that put rote facts to music: math facts, naming states and their capitals, phonic rules, and so on. Put charts on the wall for these same facts, as well, to provide regular visual reference.

3. Frequently reinforce skills and concepts being taught with games. This provides an enjoyable multi-sensory avenue for regular practice. And weak areas always need extra practice!

Reward desired behavior.

Struggling children need plenty of positive reinforcement.

1. Set small goals and continually reward his attempts to focus and achieve with specific, not vague, praise. That is, let him know you are pleased, and exactly what was done to please you. "You stayed focused for ten whole minutes!! Good for you!" followed by a hug is more specific than "Okay, good job. Let's move on." Regular, specific, sincere praise motivates children to persevere. The ultimate goal is

to teach children to monitor their own behavior. They need to develop the habit of giving themselves small goals and then patting themselves on the back as each goal is achieved. Over time this helps develop a sense of accomplishment, resulting in greater self-confidence.

2. Also use nonverbal rewards. Allow the student to earn privileges by proper behavior. Determine the privilege—what does he want to do? Play a game with you? Have some free time? Have a friend over? Then negotiate the behavior required for each privilege. The student should be part of this process in order to increase his motivation. Sometimes a written contract is helpful. When used frequently, this technique helps prevent the "poor me" attitude that can come from continual discouragement, replacing it with a sense of control.

Regularly evaluate expectations and resources.

1. If the student fails at a task be sure the instructions are understood and have him use concrete materials. If the student continues to fail despite regular help, reevaluate the appropriateness of the assignment.

   - The student may need review of background material before he will be able to understand what is now being taught. Phonics and math are subjects that frequently require review of previous concepts.

   - The student may need a greater variety of experiences before he will be able to succeed.

He may simply require a great deal of practice and repetition before he retains the concept or develops the skill. Varying experiences keep the repetition from becoming too tedious. Or, he may need experiences that make the concept more real. Reading (or listening) to a description or looking at an illustration may not have been sufficient. In that case, physical demonstrations, hands-on projects, field trips, and/or videos can provide the understanding that appears to be lacking.

- If the problem seems to be an inability to maintain attention, the length of time spent on the lesson could be decreased, replacing one long lesson with several short sessions throughout the day.

2. Provide continual and specific feedback. Point out what was done correctly, any errors, and what must be done to correct those errors.

3. Maintain a dialogue with the student. He should become comfortable telling you what he does and does not understand, sharing what seems to work ("I remembered better last time when I . . .") and even suggesting ways to try to achieve his goals. This will increase his ability to work independently as he matures. It will also increase his sense of control and self-confidence.

As a teenager, my son recognized that as much as he wanted to be around people, he accomplished more if he could severely limit distractions. One day a week he had a music lesson followed by a group lesson about an hour later. He suggested that he spend that hour in a practice room rather than returning home. At first he would telephone every five or ten minutes. I provided a sympathetic ear, and encouraged him to get back to work by suggesting specific goals. As he gradually became productive for longer periods, the phone calls decreased until they were occasional, not constant.

4. Experiment to find methods and materials effective for your specific situation. As your child matures, his needs will change. Determine priorities according to his age and future goals.

Give yourself a break.

1. Look for outside services that can help your child— speech therapy, occupational therapy, art or music lessons, physical education classes, and/or youth group activities. These provide the child with valuable experiences and remove a bit of planning and instruction time from your schedule.

2. Find time every day to do something that will refresh you so that you can continue to be the patient and positive influence the child needs.

3. Keep your eyes on the long-term goal whenever you become discouraged. Remind yourself of the importance of what you are doing.

4. Think about the child's good qualities to help offset the frustrations of the day.

Resources

The companies listed below carry materials appropriate for meeting special needs. Write or call to request a catalog.

Academic Therapy Publications
Phone 1-800-422-7249   www.atpub.com
20 Commercial Boulevard, Novato, CA 94949-6191
Academic Therapy Publications. Books and materials for assessments, visual remediation, parent or teacher guidance, and other curriculum supplements.
High Noon Books. Books with low readability levels (grades 1-4 reading levels) but with content appropriate to cover objectives through the high school level.

ADD Warehouse
Phone 1-800-233-9273   www.addwarehouse.com
300 N.W. 70th Avenue, Suite 102, Plantation, FL 33317
Videos, books, and supplies for understanding and treating ADD/ADHD and other special needs.

AGS Instructional Materials & Tests
Phone 1-800-328-2560   www.agsnet.com
P.O. Box 99, Circle Pines, MN 55014-1796
Elementary Catalog: tests, materials for behavior/social skills, early childhood, speech and language skills, and parenting. *Secondary Catalog*: tests, basic skill texts in all major subjects (some with lower-level reading abilities), consumer math, work skills, social skills, and GED preparation materials.

Attainment Company
Phone 1-800-327-4269   www.attainmentcompany.com
P.O. Box 930160, Verona, WI 53593-0160
Materials, including software, to develop life skills.

Calloway House
Phone 1-800-233-0290   www.callowayhouse.com
451 Richardson Drive, Lancaster, PA 17603-4098
Materials include cardboard partitions for study carrels
and a variety of games and manipulatives for language
arts, math, and science.

Communication / Therapy Skill Builders
Phone 1-800-211-8378   www.hbtpc.com
The Psychological Corporation, 555 Academic Court,
San Antonio, TX 78204-2498
Assessment; *Communication Skill Builders*—speech and
language resources; *Therapy Skill Builders*—
occupational therapy, managing behavior, hands-on
materials.

Continental Press
Phone 1-800-233-0759   www.continentalpress.com
520 E. Bainbridge St., Elizabethtown, PA 17022
Literacy skills, test preparation workbooks, and
materials in other subjects, K-12.

Design-A-Study
Phone (302) 998-3889   www.designastudy.com
408 Victoria Ave., Wilmington, DE 19804-2124
Titles mentioned throughout this book are available
here. *Natural Speller* has a multi-sensory approach
recommended for children with difficulty in this area.

ECS Learning Systems, Inc.
Phone 1-800-688-3224 www.educyberstor.com
P.O. Box 791439, San Antonio, TX 78279-1439
While not specifically for special needs, this catalog includes software to build basic skills sequentially as well as books with hands-on activities.

ECL Publications
Phone 1-877-974-4560 www.eclpublications.com
P.O. Box 26, Youngtown, AZ 85363
Resources for developing speech and language skills.

Educators Publishing Service, Inc.
Phone 1-800-225-5750 www.epsbooks.com
31 Smith Place, Cambridge, MA 02138-1089
K-12 catalog includes multi-sensory programs for teaching reading to children with a variety of learning disabilities.

ESP Publishers, Inc.
Phone 1-800-643-0280 www.espbooks.com
7100 123rd Circle North #100, Largo, FL 33773
Consumable textbooks for low functioning junior and senior high school students.

Gamco
Phone 1-800-351-1404 www.gamco.com
P.O. Box 50189, St. Louis, M) 63144
Software and videos for special needs K-12.

hach
Phone 1-800-624-7968 www.hachstuff.com
P.O. Box 11927, Winston-Salem, NC 27116

An early childhood catalog with furniture, learning toys, books, and K-3rd grade subjects in software for special needs children—nonvocal, limited physical mobility, autistic, dyslexic, and even those functioning below nine months of age.

Imaginart
Phone 1-800-828-1376 www.imaginartonline.com
307 Arizona Street, Bisbee, AZ 85603
Catalog for communication offers products for ages infant through elderly. Catalog for therapy products includes resources for occupational therapy.

I-MED
(Instructional Materials & Equipment Distributors)
Phone (323) 879-0377
1520 Cotner Ave., Los Angeles, CA 90001
Request the catalog for perceptual communication skills

J. Weston Walch Publisher
Phone 1-800-341-6094 www.walch.com
P.O. Box 658, Portland, ME 04104-0658
Catalog for Middle School – Adult includes curriculum materials with lower-level readability, behavior/social skills, work skills, and independent living.

Janelle Publications
Phone 1-800-888-8834 www.janellepublications.com
P.O. Box 811, 1189 Twombley Rd., DeKalb, IL 60115
Speech and language materials for basic skills—young children or special needs.

Learning Services
Phone *West* 1-800-877-9378 *East* 1-800-877-3278
www.learnserv.com
P.O. Box 10636, Eugene, OR 97440-2636
Software, preschool – 12 in all subjects. Includes
software for narrow, specific, academic needs—just
practicing long and short vowels, or practice with
decimals, for example.

**Mayer-Johnson Company – Augmentative
Communication Products**
Phone 1-800-588-4548 www.mayer-johnson.com
P.O. Box 1579, Solana Beach, CA 92075
Special needs resources include communication devices,
software, and books.

NATHHAN
Phone 208-267-6246 www.NATHHAN.com
P.O. Box 39, Porthill, ID 83853
Besides selling materials for speech and reading, they
offer a special needs newsletter and access to their 500-
volume lending library.

PRO-ED
Phone 1-800-897-3202 www.proedinc.com
8700 Shoal Creek Boulevard, Austin, TX 78757
Specify catalog: *Special Ed*; *Speech, Language, and
Hearing*; and/or *Psychological Products*.

R J Cooper & Associates
Phone 1-800-RJCOOPER www.rjcooper.com.
24843 Del Prado #283, Dana Point, CA 92629
Special software and hardware adaptations for severe
disabilities.

Simplified Learning Products
Phone/Fax 1-800-745-8212   www.joyceherzog.com
P.O. Box 45387, Rio Rancho, NM 87174-5387
Includes the *Scaredy Cat Reading System* developed
especially to meet special needs, and a book on choosing
curriculum, both by Joyce Herzog.

The Speech Bin
Phone 1-800-4-SPEECH
1965 Twenty-Fifth Avenue, Vero Beach, FL 32960
Includes materials for speech and language,
occupational and physical therapy, and various special
needs—autism, down syndrome, communication
disorders.

Super Duper Publications
Phone 1-800-277-8737   www.superduperinc.com
P.O. Box 24997, Greenville, SC 29616
Speech and language development materials including
items especially for those with limited or no speech.
Materials for working with autism include strategies for
dealing with behavior.

A FINAL REMINDER

It's easy to become so focused on a problem that you forget that the child has any strengths or talents at all.

- Reflect on the good things.

- Recall his successes.

- Remember his hugs.

- Remind yourself that he has a purpose.

And, above all, realize that you are doing more than solving a problem. **By your words and actions, you are teaching your child how to face life's difficulties.** Let trials turn into blessings.

ADDITIONAL HELP FROM THE AUTHOR

Free Monthly Teaching Help Column More teaching tips by Kathryn Stout are available at the Design-A-Study website: www.designastudy.com

Her Design-A-Study Books

Comprehensive Composition

Just one volume covers grades K-12. Teaching tips include an easy-to-use strategy encouraging better writing through editing, allowing students to develop at their own pace and improve with practice. Eliminate boredom by choosing the type of composition and an appealing topic from among those listed which suit the student's needs and interests. Subjects include paragraphs, essays, reports, outlines, narratives, biographies, letters, short stories; persuasive, descriptive, expository and creative writing; choosing and narrowing a topic; content and structure skills; mechanics and sample lessons. Use it alone or as a reference. Recommended by Cathy Duffy as "One of the most concise yet comprehensive books for teaching the writing process available to home educators." $14.00

Critical Conditioning

Now you can see all of the K-12 components of reading comprehension, along with definitions, explanations, and activity ideas. Teaching tips include ways to incorporate analysis and thinking skills while covering comprehension objectives. Topics include elements and types of literature, reference skills, SQRRR study skills, propaganda techniques, discussion questions, and more. This is an area too easily forgotten when library books are used as the reading program. For anyone using readers, this helps eliminate the busy work. $12.00

Natural Speller

The only book you will ever need to teach spelling. Lists for grades 1 through 8. Latin and Greek roots and word lists can be used to build vocabulary in higher grades as well. Word lists are organized by both sight and sound patterns for use with students having difficulty with long-term retention. Includes phonics, spelling, and punctuation rules, as well as teaching tips. Activities include practice with grammar, dictionary, and composition skills. Each child can work at his own pace. Recommended by Dr. Ruth Beechick. $22.00

Maximum Math

The ultimate guide to teaching math in grades K-8. Fill in gaps; allow students to progress as far as ability permits. Teaching tips offer ideas for working with all learning styles to promote understanding of concepts and increase problem solving ability. Graded objectives conform to NCTM standards and are arranged to allow you to follow an objective over several grades. Activities are provided for initial instruction. Just add a few manipulatives to teach grades K-2. Supplement grades 3-8 with practice problems using software, workbooks, texts, kits, and/or games. $24.00

Science Scope

Concepts and skills taught in grades K-12 are arranged for easy teaching of multi-levels or to allow a child to progress as far as he is able in any area. Teach the scientific process. Use a variety of fun and interesting resources without fear of leaving educational gaps. Teaching strategies include tips to help children think scientifically and get the most out of their explorations and experiences. A checklist allows convenient record keeping. Students in grades 6-12 can use it as a working outline to find information on their own. $15.00.

Guides to History Plus

Social studies objectives—American and world history, geography, government, and economics—are incorporated into an easy-to-use question guide for the study of any period or culture in grades K-12. Also useful for an independent study. Activity ideas incorporate objectives in other subjects for those interested in a unit study approach to history. Also included: teaching tips, instructions for making timelines, lists of map skills, reproducible blank maps, definitions of geographic terms, questions to provide practice in analysis for high school students, lists of literature, games, and movies on video arranged by period and topic for grades 6-12; and grade 9-12 objectives for those developing transcripts. $14.00.

The Maya

A complete unit study on this advanced, ancient, American civilization. Since this information and specific activity ideas follow the outline in the *Guides to History Plus*, this unit can also serve as a model for making your own historical study. $5.00

Audiocassettes of "How-To" Workshops
$4.50 each or $4.00 each when purchasing 3 or more.

Make It Easy On Yourself. Put the spark back into your homeschool! Turn your kids into thinkers and independent learners without exhausting *yourself* or your checking account. Here are teaching strategies and resource ideas guaranteed to keep kids excited about learning and make it all run smoothly. 90 min

Developing Attitudes and Habits: What's Important & When There's a best time for developing the attitudes and habits that affect not only a child's character, but also his ability to learn beyond high school. Includes specific goals, teaching strategies, and techniques to replace bad habits with good ones. 60 min.

Teaching Kids to Think How to stress reasoning, problem solving, and supporting opinions while covering objectives in reading comprehension, composition, and science. 60 min.

How to Teach Composition   Every child should be able to express himself logically and succinctly.   Teach clarity of thought as part of the writing process, Tips include keys to evaluation so that you can help your child build skill instead of simply complete assignments.   60 min

Teaching English: What's Essential?   Do your children dig beyond the basic plot, analyzing, appreciating, and learning life lessons from literature?   Tips include what to emphasize and when in order to teach children to do such that and to compose interesting and well-supported essays that reflect their ability to think critically.   60 min.

Teaching Teenagers to Think Critically   Arm your teens with protection from worldly propaganda.   Easily incorporated into basic subjects, these strategies build skills in analyzing what is read, watched, and heard.   60 min

Strategies for Teaching & Learning Spelling   Here are the tools needed to learn and retain correct selling.   These strategies build confident learners and teachers.   45 min.

Math That Makes Sense   Tips for teaching math concepts to grades K-8 that promote discovery and reasoning.   45 min

Teaching Reading, Spelling & Critical Thinking   Help children see patterns and use reasoning.   60 min

A Chronological Unit Approach to History   Give students a chance to understand and enjoy history. Use nonfiction books that have kid-appeal, literature that broadens their perspective, and enjoyable activities that leave them with English skills that would have otherwise been tedious to acquire. Includes ideas for relating other subjects to history.   45 min.

Teaching Tips That Really Work   How to overcome the "I can't, I won't" syndrome, teach through strengths, build up weak areas, and create a problem-solving atmosphere.   Includes advice for handling common problems.   60 min.

Resources are available from Design-A-Study, 408 Victoria Ave., Wilmington, DE 19804-2124. Phone/Fax (302) 998-3889.